THE PRAYER MAP®

FOR A "Moving Mountains" Kind of Girl

FOR WOMEN OF ALL AGES

Print ISBN 979-8-89151-111-8

Published by Barbour Publishing, Inc., 1810 Barbour Drive, Uhrichsville, Ohio 44683, www.barbourbooks.com

Our mission is to inspire the world with the life-changing message of the Bible.

Printed in China.

Get Ready to Move Some Mountains in Your Prayer Life, Girl!

Get ready to experience the power of courageous prayer in your everyday life with this creative journal. . .where every colorful page will guide you to create your very own prayer map—as you write out specific thoughts, ideas, and lists, which you can follow (from start to finish!) as you talk to God. (Be sure to record the date on each one of your prayer maps so you can look back over time and see how God has continued to work in your life!)

The Prayer Map for a "Moving Mountains" Kind of Girl will not only encourage you to pray bold, confident prayers. . .it will also help you build a healthy spiritual habit of continual prayer for life!

Date:

DEAR HEAVENLY FATHER,

I believe mountains can move.

THIS IS WHAT NEEDS MOVING IN MY LIFE TODAY. . .

HERE IS WHERE I'M STRUGGLING IN MY FAITH. . .

PLEASE ERASE ANY DOUBT IN MY HEART SO THAT. . .

WITH YOU BY MY SIDE, *I know*. . .

is possible.

I trust You to. . .

TOGETHER, YOU AND I CAN MOVE THOSE MOUNTAINS, LORD!

Thank You, Father, for hearing my prayers! **AMEN.**

"I tell you the truth, you can say to this mountain, 'May you be lifted up and thrown into the sea,' and it will happen. But you must really believe it will happen and have no doubt in your heart."

MARK 11:23 NLT

Date:

DEAR HEAVENLY FATHER,

I believe mountains can move.

THIS IS WHAT NEEDS MOVING IN MY LIFE TODAY. . .

HERE IS WHERE I'M STRUGGLING IN MY FAITH. . .

PLEASE ERASE ANY DOUBT IN MY HEART SO THAT. . .

WITH YOU BY MY SIDE, *I know*. . .

is possible.

I trust You to. . .

TOGETHER, YOU AND I CAN MOVE THOSE MOUNTAINS, LORD!

Thank You, Father, for hearing my prayers! **AMEN.**

When doubts filled my mind, your comfort gave me renewed hope and cheer.

PSALM 94:19 NLT

Date:

DEAR HEAVENLY FATHER,

I believe mountains can move.

THIS IS WHAT NEEDS MOVING IN MY LIFE TODAY. . .

HERE IS WHERE I'M STRUGGLING IN MY FAITH. . .

PLEASE ERASE ANY DOUBT IN MY HEART SO THAT. . .

WITH YOU BY MY SIDE, *I know. . .*

is possible.

I trust You to. . .

TOGETHER, YOU AND I CAN MOVE THOSE MOUNTAINS, LORD!

Thank You, Father, for hearing my prayers! **AMEN.**

[Jesus] said. . . , "Put your finger into My hands. Put your hand into My side. Do not doubt, believe!"

John 20:27 NLV

Date:

DEAR HEAVENLY FATHER,

I believe mountains can move.

THIS IS WHAT NEEDS MOVING IN MY LIFE TODAY. . .

HERE IS WHERE I'M STRUGGLING IN MY FAITH. . .

PLEASE ERASE ANY DOUBT IN MY HEART SO THAT. . .

WITH YOU BY MY SIDE, *I know*. . .

is possible.

I trust You to. . .

TOGETHER, YOU AND I CAN MOVE THOSE MOUNTAINS, LORD!

Thank You, Father, for hearing my prayers! **AMEN.**

You must have faith as you ask Him.
You must not doubt. Anyone who doubts is like
a wave which is pushed around by the sea.
JAMES 1:6 NLV

Date:

DEAR HEAVENLY FATHER,

I believe mountains can move.

THIS IS WHAT NEEDS MOVING IN MY LIFE TODAY. . .

HERE IS WHERE I'M STRUGGLING IN MY FAITH. . .

PLEASE ERASE ANY DOUBT IN MY HEART SO THAT. . .

WITH YOU BY MY SIDE, *I know. . .*

is possible.

I trust You to. . .

TOGETHER, YOU AND I CAN MOVE THOSE MOUNTAINS, LORD!

Thank You, Father, for hearing my prayers! **AMEN.**

Have loving-kindness for those who doubt.

JUDE 1:22 NLV

Date:

DEAR HEAVENLY FATHER,

I believe mountains can move.

THIS IS WHAT NEEDS MOVING IN MY LIFE TODAY. . .

HERE IS WHERE I'M STRUGGLING IN MY FAITH. . .

PLEASE ERASE ANY DOUBT IN MY HEART SO THAT. . .

WITH YOU BY MY SIDE, *I know. . .* ....

....

....

....

....

.... *is possible.*

I trust You to. . .

....

....

....

....

....

....

TOGETHER, YOU AND I CAN MOVE THOSE MOUNTAINS, LORD!

Thank You, Father, for hearing my prayers! **AMEN.**

But the wisdom that comes from heaven. . .
gives peace. It is gentle and willing to obey. It is full of
loving-kindness and of doing good. It has no doubts
and does not pretend to be something it is not.

JAMES 3:17 NLV

Date:

DEAR HEAVENLY FATHER,

I believe mountains can move.

THIS IS WHAT NEEDS MOVING IN MY LIFE TODAY. . .

HERE IS WHERE I'M STRUGGLING IN MY FAITH. . .

PLEASE ERASE ANY DOUBT IN MY HEART SO THAT. . .

WITH YOU BY MY SIDE, *I know. . .* ....

....

....

....

....

.... *is possible.*

I trust You to. . .

....

....

....

....

....

....

TOGETHER, YOU AND I CAN MOVE THOSE MOUNTAINS, LORD!

Thank You, Father, for hearing my prayers! **AMEN.**

"I do believe; help me overcome my unbelief!"
MARK 9:24 NIV

Date:

DEAR HEAVENLY FATHER,

I believe mountains can move.

THIS IS WHAT NEEDS MOVING IN MY LIFE TODAY. . .

HERE IS WHERE I'M STRUGGLING IN MY FAITH. . .

PLEASE ERASE ANY DOUBT IN MY HEART SO THAT. . .

WITH YOU BY MY SIDE, *I know. . .*

is possible.

I trust You to. . .

TOGETHER, YOU AND I CAN MOVE THOSE MOUNTAINS, LORD!

Thank You, Father, for hearing my prayers! **AMEN.**

Be anxious for nothing, but in everything by prayer and supplication, with thanksgiving, let your requests be made known to God; and the peace of God, which surpasses all understanding, will guard your hearts and minds through Christ Jesus.

PHILIPPIANS 4:6–7 NKJV

Date:

DEAR HEAVENLY FATHER,

I believe mountains can move.

THIS IS WHAT NEEDS MOVING IN MY LIFE TODAY. . .

HERE IS WHERE I'M STRUGGLING IN MY FAITH. . .

PLEASE ERASE ANY DOUBT IN MY HEART SO THAT. . .

WITH YOU BY MY SIDE, *I know*. . .

is possible.

I trust You to. . .

TOGETHER, YOU AND I CAN MOVE THOSE MOUNTAINS, LORD!

Thank You, Father, for hearing my prayers! **AMEN.**

Search me, God, and know my heart;
test me and know my anxious thoughts.
PSALM 139:23 NIV

Date:

DEAR HEAVENLY FATHER,

I believe mountains can move.

THIS IS WHAT NEEDS MOVING IN MY LIFE TODAY. . .

HERE IS WHERE I'M STRUGGLING IN MY FAITH. . .

PLEASE ERASE ANY DOUBT IN MY HEART SO THAT. . .

WITH YOU BY MY SIDE, I know. . .

is possible.

I trust You to. . .

TOGETHER, YOU AND I CAN MOVE THOSE MOUNTAINS, LORD!

Thank You, Father, for hearing my prayers! **AMEN.**

May God bless you richly and grant you increasing freedom from all anxiety and fear.
1 PETER 1:2 TLB

Date:

DEAR HEAVENLY FATHER,

I believe mountains can move.

THIS IS WHAT NEEDS MOVING IN MY LIFE TODAY. . .

HERE IS WHERE I'M STRUGGLING IN MY FAITH. . .

PLEASE ERASE ANY DOUBT IN MY HEART SO THAT. . .

WITH YOU BY MY SIDE, *I know*. . .

is possible.

I trust You to. . .

TOGETHER, YOU AND I CAN MOVE THOSE MOUNTAINS, LORD!

Thank You, Father, for hearing my prayers! **AMEN.**

"Do not be anxious about your life, what you will eat or what you will drink, nor about your body, what you will put on. Is not life more than food, and the body more than clothing?"

MATTHEW 6:25 ESV

Date:

DEAR HEAVENLY FATHER,

I believe mountains can move.

THIS IS WHAT NEEDS MOVING IN MY LIFE TODAY. . .

HERE IS WHERE I'M STRUGGLING IN MY FAITH. . .

PLEASE ERASE ANY DOUBT IN MY HEART SO THAT. . .

WITH YOU BY MY SIDE, *I know*. . .

is possible.

I trust You to. . .

TOGETHER, YOU AND I CAN MOVE THOSE MOUNTAINS, LORD!

Thank You, Father, for hearing my prayers! **AMEN.**

"For he shall be like a tree planted by the waters, which spreads out its roots by the river, and will not fear when heat comes; but its leaf will be green, and will not be anxious in the year of drought, nor will cease from yielding fruit."

JEREMIAH 17:8 NKJV

Date:

DEAR HEAVENLY FATHER,

I believe mountains can move.

THIS IS WHAT NEEDS MOVING IN MY LIFE TODAY. . .

HERE IS WHERE I'M STRUGGLING IN MY FAITH. . .

PLEASE ERASE ANY DOUBT IN MY HEART SO THAT. . .

WITH YOU BY MY SIDE, *I know. . .*

is possible.

I trust You to. . .

TOGETHER, YOU AND I CAN MOVE THOSE MOUNTAINS, LORD!

Thank You, Father, for hearing my prayers! **AMEN.**

Anxiety weighs down the heart,
but a kind word cheers it up.
PROVERBS 12:25 NIV

Date: ....

DEAR HEAVENLY FATHER, ...

I believe mountains can move.

THIS IS WHAT NEEDS MOVING IN MY LIFE TODAY. . .

HERE IS WHERE I'M STRUGGLING IN MY FAITH. . .

PLEASE ERASE ANY DOUBT IN MY HEART SO THAT. . .

WITH YOU BY MY SIDE, *I know. . .* ....

....

....

....

....

.... *is possible.*

I trust You to. . .

....

....

....

....

....

....

TOGETHER, YOU AND I CAN MOVE THOSE MOUNTAINS, LORD!

Thank You, Father, for hearing my prayers! **AMEN.**

Do not be afraid of those who hate you.
Their hate for you proves they will be destroyed.
It proves you have life from God that lasts forever.
PHILIPPIANS 1:28 NLV

Date:

DEAR HEAVENLY FATHER,

I believe mountains can move.

THIS IS WHAT NEEDS MOVING IN MY LIFE TODAY. . .

HERE IS WHERE I'M STRUGGLING IN MY FAITH. . .

PLEASE ERASE ANY DOUBT IN MY HEART SO THAT. . .

WITH YOU BY MY SIDE, *I know. . .* ....

....

....

....

....

.... *is possible.*

I trust You to. . .

....

....

....

....

....

....

TOGETHER, YOU AND I CAN MOVE THOSE MOUNTAINS, LORD!

Thank You, Father, for hearing my prayers! **AMEN.**

Say to those who have an anxious heart,
"Be strong; fear not! Behold, your God will
come with vengeance, with the recompense
of God. He will come and save you."

ISAIAH 35:4 ESV

Date:

DEAR HEAVENLY FATHER,

I believe mountains can move.

THIS IS WHAT NEEDS MOVING IN MY LIFE TODAY. . .

HERE IS WHERE I'M STRUGGLING IN MY FAITH. . .

PLEASE ERASE ANY DOUBT IN MY HEART SO THAT. . .

WITH YOU BY MY SIDE, *I know*. . .

is possible.

I trust You to. . .

TOGETHER, YOU AND I CAN MOVE THOSE MOUNTAINS, LORD!

Thank You, Father, for hearing my prayers! **AMEN.**

"Be strong and courageous. Do not fear or be in dread of them, for it is the L*ORD* *your God who goes with you. He will not leave you or forsake you."*

DEUTERONOMY 31:6 ESV

Date:

DEAR HEAVENLY FATHER,

I believe mountains can move.

THIS IS WHAT NEEDS MOVING IN MY LIFE TODAY. . .

HERE IS WHERE I'M STRUGGLING IN MY FAITH. . .

PLEASE ERASE ANY DOUBT IN MY HEART SO THAT. . .

WITH YOU BY MY SIDE, I know. . .

is possible.

I trust You to. . .

TOGETHER, YOU AND I CAN MOVE THOSE MOUNTAINS, LORD!

Thank You, Father, for hearing my prayers! **AMEN.**

"But you, take courage! Do not let your hands be weak, for your work shall be rewarded."
2 Chronicles 15:7 ESV

Date:

DEAR HEAVENLY FATHER,

I believe mountains can move.

THIS IS WHAT NEEDS MOVING IN MY LIFE TODAY. . .

HERE IS WHERE I'M STRUGGLING IN MY FAITH. . .

PLEASE ERASE ANY DOUBT IN MY HEART SO THAT. . .

WITH YOU BY MY SIDE, *I know*. . .

is possible.

I trust You to. . .

TOGETHER, YOU AND I CAN MOVE THOSE MOUNTAINS, LORD!

Thank You, Father, for hearing my prayers! **AMEN.**

Be strong, be courageous,
all you that hope in the LORD.
PSALM 31:24 GNT

Date:

DEAR HEAVENLY FATHER,

I believe mountains can move.

THIS IS WHAT NEEDS MOVING IN MY LIFE TODAY. . .

HERE IS WHERE I'M STRUGGLING IN MY FAITH. . .

PLEASE ERASE ANY DOUBT IN MY HEART SO THAT. . .

WITH YOU BY MY SIDE, *I know. . .* ....

....

....

....

....

.... *is possible.*

I trust You to. . .

....

....

....

....

....

....

TOGETHER, YOU AND I CAN MOVE THOSE MOUNTAINS, LORD!

Thank You, Father, for hearing my prayers! **AMEN.**

Be on your guard; stand firm in the faith; be courageous; be strong.

1 CORINTHIANS 16:13 NIV

Date:

DEAR HEAVENLY FATHER,

I believe mountains can move.

THIS IS WHAT NEEDS MOVING IN MY LIFE TODAY. . .

HERE IS WHERE I'M STRUGGLING IN MY FAITH. . .

PLEASE ERASE ANY DOUBT IN MY HEART SO THAT. . .

WITH YOU BY MY SIDE, *I know*. . .

is possible.

I trust You to. . .

TOGETHER, YOU AND I CAN MOVE THOSE MOUNTAINS, LORD!

Thank You, Father, for hearing my prayers! **AMEN.**

I cling to you; your strong
right hand holds me securely.
PSALM 63:8 NLT

Date:

DEAR HEAVENLY FATHER,

I believe mountains can move.

THIS IS WHAT NEEDS MOVING IN MY LIFE TODAY. . .

HERE IS WHERE I'M STRUGGLING IN MY FAITH. . .

PLEASE ERASE ANY DOUBT IN MY HEART SO THAT. . .

WITH YOU BY MY SIDE, *I know*. . .

is possible.

I trust You to. . .

TOGETHER, YOU AND I CAN MOVE THOSE MOUNTAINS, LORD!

Thank You, Father, for hearing my prayers! **AMEN.**

I praise you, for I am fearfully and wonderfully made. Wonderful are your works; my soul knows it very well.

PSALM 139:14 ESV

Date:

DEAR HEAVENLY FATHER,

I believe mountains can move.

THIS IS WHAT NEEDS MOVING IN MY LIFE TODAY. . .

HERE IS WHERE I'M STRUGGLING IN MY FAITH. . .

PLEASE ERASE ANY DOUBT IN MY HEART SO THAT. . .

WITH YOU BY MY SIDE, *I know. . .*

is possible.

I trust You to. . .

TOGETHER, YOU AND I CAN MOVE THOSE MOUNTAINS, LORD!

Thank You, Father, for hearing my prayers! **AMEN.**

Do not be conformed to this world, but be transformed by the renewal of your mind, that by testing you may discern what is the will of God, what is good and acceptable and perfect.

ROMANS 12:2 ESV

Date:

DEAR HEAVENLY FATHER,

I believe mountains can move.

THIS IS WHAT NEEDS MOVING IN MY LIFE TODAY. . .

HERE IS WHERE I'M STRUGGLING IN MY FAITH. . .

PLEASE ERASE ANY DOUBT IN MY HEART SO THAT. . .

WITH YOU BY MY SIDE, *I know. . .*

is possible.

I trust You to. . .

TOGETHER, YOU AND I CAN MOVE THOSE MOUNTAINS, LORD!

Thank You, Father, for hearing my prayers! **AMEN.**

"And you will feel secure, because there is hope;
you will look around and take your rest in security."
JOB 11:18 ESV

Date:

DEAR HEAVENLY FATHER,

I believe mountains can move.

THIS IS WHAT NEEDS MOVING IN MY LIFE TODAY. . .

HERE IS WHERE I'M STRUGGLING IN MY FAITH. . .

PLEASE ERASE ANY DOUBT IN MY HEART SO THAT. . .

WITH YOU BY MY SIDE, *I know. . .* ....

....

....

....

....

.... *is possible.*

I trust You to. . .

....

....

....

....

....

....

TOGETHER, YOU AND I CAN MOVE THOSE MOUNTAINS, LORD!

Thank You, Father, for hearing my prayers! **AMEN.**

"I will bring health and healing to [the city of Jerusalem]; I will heal my people and will let them enjoy abundant peace and security."

JEREMIAH 33:6 NIV

Date:

DEAR HEAVENLY FATHER,

I believe mountains can move.

THIS IS WHAT NEEDS MOVING IN MY LIFE TODAY. . .

HERE IS WHERE I'M STRUGGLING IN MY FAITH. . .

PLEASE ERASE ANY DOUBT IN MY HEART SO THAT. . .

WITH YOU BY MY SIDE, *I know. . .*

is possible.

I trust You to. . .

TOGETHER, YOU AND I CAN MOVE THOSE MOUNTAINS, LORD!

Thank You, Father, for hearing my prayers! **AMEN.**

He pulled me out of a dangerous pit,
out of the deadly quicksand. He set me
safely on a rock and made me secure.

PSALM 40:2 GNT

Date:

DEAR HEAVENLY FATHER,

I believe mountains can move.

THIS IS WHAT NEEDS MOVING IN MY LIFE TODAY. . .

HERE IS WHERE I'M STRUGGLING IN MY FAITH. . .

PLEASE ERASE ANY DOUBT IN MY HEART SO THAT. . .

WITH YOU BY MY SIDE, *I know*. . .

is possible.

I trust You to. . .

TOGETHER, YOU AND I CAN MOVE THOSE MOUNTAINS, LORD!

Thank You, Father, for hearing my prayers! **AMEN.**

And you also became God's people when you heard the true message, the Good News that brought you salvation. You believed in Christ, and God put his stamp of ownership on you by giving you the Holy Spirit he had promised.

EPHESIANS 1:13 GNT

Date:

DEAR HEAVENLY FATHER,

I believe mountains can move.

THIS IS WHAT NEEDS MOVING IN MY LIFE TODAY. . .

HERE IS WHERE I'M STRUGGLING IN MY FAITH. . .

PLEASE ERASE ANY DOUBT IN MY HEART SO THAT. . .

WITH YOU BY MY SIDE, *I know. . .* ....

....

....

....

....

.... *is possible.*

I trust You to. . .

....

....

....

....

....

....

TOGETHER, YOU AND I CAN MOVE THOSE MOUNTAINS, LORD!

Thank You, Father, for hearing my prayers! **AMEN.**

He heals the brokenhearted and binds up their wounds.

PSALM 147:3 ESV

Date:

DEAR HEAVENLY FATHER,

I believe mountains can move.

THIS IS WHAT NEEDS MOVING IN MY LIFE TODAY. . .

HERE IS WHERE I'M STRUGGLING IN MY FAITH. . .

PLEASE ERASE ANY DOUBT IN MY HEART SO THAT. . .

WITH YOU BY MY SIDE, *I know. . .*

is possible.

I trust You to. . .

TOGETHER, YOU AND I CAN MOVE THOSE MOUNTAINS, LORD!

Thank You, Father, for hearing my prayers! **AMEN.**

And my God will supply every need of yours according to his riches in glory in Christ Jesus.

PHILIPPIANS 4:19 ESV

Date:

DEAR HEAVENLY FATHER,

I believe mountains can move.

THIS IS WHAT NEEDS MOVING IN MY LIFE TODAY. . .

HERE IS WHERE I'M STRUGGLING IN MY FAITH. . .

PLEASE ERASE ANY DOUBT IN MY HEART SO THAT. . .

WITH YOU BY MY SIDE, *I know. . .*

is possible.

I trust You to. . .

TOGETHER, YOU AND I CAN MOVE THOSE MOUNTAINS, LORD!

Thank You, Father, for hearing my prayers! **AMEN.**

"For the LORD will not forsake his people, for his great name's sake, because it has pleased the Lord to make you a people for himself."

1 SAMUEL 12:22 ESV

Date:

DEAR HEAVENLY FATHER,

I believe mountains can move.

THIS IS WHAT NEEDS MOVING IN MY LIFE TODAY. . .

HERE IS WHERE I'M STRUGGLING IN MY FAITH. . .

PLEASE ERASE ANY DOUBT IN MY HEART SO THAT. . .

WITH YOU BY MY SIDE, *I know. . .*

is possible.

I trust You to. . .

TOGETHER, YOU AND I CAN MOVE THOSE MOUNTAINS, LORD!

Thank You, Father, for hearing my prayers! **AMEN.**

"Be sure of this: I am with you always, even to the end of the age."

MATTHEW 28:20 NLT

Date:

DEAR HEAVENLY FATHER,

I believe mountains can move.

THIS IS WHAT NEEDS MOVING IN MY LIFE TODAY. . .

HERE IS WHERE I'M STRUGGLING IN MY FAITH. . .

PLEASE ERASE ANY DOUBT IN MY HEART SO THAT. . .

WITH YOU BY MY SIDE, *I know*. . .

is possible.

I trust You to. . .

TOGETHER, YOU AND I CAN MOVE THOSE MOUNTAINS, LORD!

Thank You, Father, for hearing my prayers! **AMEN.**

Turn to me, LORD, and be merciful to me, because I am lonely and weak.

PSALM 25:16 GNT

Date:

DEAR HEAVENLY FATHER,

I believe mountains can move.

THIS IS WHAT NEEDS MOVING IN MY LIFE TODAY. . .

HERE IS WHERE I'M STRUGGLING IN MY FAITH. . .

PLEASE ERASE ANY DOUBT IN MY HEART SO THAT. . .

WITH YOU BY MY SIDE, *I know*. . .

is possible.

I trust You to. . .

TOGETHER, YOU AND I CAN MOVE THOSE MOUNTAINS, LORD!

Thank You, Father, for hearing my prayers! **AMEN.**

They do not fear bad news; they confidently trust the L*ORD* *to care for them.*

PSALM 112:7 NLT

Date:

DEAR HEAVENLY FATHER,

I believe mountains can move.

THIS IS WHAT NEEDS MOVING IN MY LIFE TODAY. . .

HERE IS WHERE I'M STRUGGLING IN MY FAITH. . .

PLEASE ERASE ANY DOUBT IN MY HEART SO THAT. . .

WITH YOU BY MY SIDE, *I know. . .* ....

....

....

....

....

.... *is possible.*

I trust You to. . .

....

....

....

....

....

....

TOGETHER, YOU AND I CAN MOVE THOSE MOUNTAINS, LORD!

Thank You, Father, for hearing my prayers! **AMEN.**

Some trust in chariots and some in horses,
but we trust in the name of the LORD *our God.*

PSALM 20:7 ESV

Date:

DEAR HEAVENLY FATHER,

I believe mountains can move.

THIS IS WHAT NEEDS MOVING IN MY LIFE TODAY. . .

HERE IS WHERE I'M STRUGGLING IN MY FAITH. . .

PLEASE ERASE ANY DOUBT IN MY HEART SO THAT. . .

WITH YOU BY MY SIDE, *I know. . .* ....

....

....

....

....

.... *is possible.*

I trust You to. . .

....

....

....

....

....

....

TOGETHER, YOU AND I CAN MOVE THOSE MOUNTAINS, LORD!

Thank You, Father, for hearing my prayers! **AMEN.**

You will keep in perfect peace those whose minds are steadfast, because they trust in you. Trust in the Lord *forever, for the* Lord, *the* Lord *himself, is the Rock eternal.*

Isaiah 26:3–4 niv

Date:

DEAR HEAVENLY FATHER,

I believe mountains can move.

THIS IS WHAT NEEDS MOVING IN MY LIFE TODAY. . .

HERE IS WHERE I'M STRUGGLING IN MY FAITH. . .

PLEASE ERASE ANY DOUBT IN MY HEART SO THAT. . .

WITH YOU BY MY SIDE, *I know. . .*

is possible.

I trust You to. . .

TOGETHER, YOU AND I CAN MOVE THOSE MOUNTAINS, LORD!

Thank You, Father, for hearing my prayers! **AMEN.**

When I am afraid, I put my trust in you. In God, whose word I praise—in God I trust and am not afraid. What can mere mortals do to me?

PSALM 56:3–4 NIV

Date:

DEAR HEAVENLY FATHER,

I believe mountains can move.

THIS IS WHAT NEEDS MOVING IN MY LIFE TODAY. . .

HERE IS WHERE I'M STRUGGLING IN MY FAITH. . .

PLEASE ERASE ANY DOUBT IN MY HEART SO THAT. . .

WITH YOU BY MY SIDE, *I know. . .*

is possible.

I trust You to. . .

TOGETHER, YOU AND I CAN MOVE THOSE MOUNTAINS, LORD!

Thank You, Father, for hearing my prayers! **AMEN.**

Commit your way to the Lord;
trust in him, and he will act.
Psalm 37:5 ESV

Date:

DEAR HEAVENLY FATHER,

I believe mountains can move.

THIS IS WHAT NEEDS MOVING IN MY LIFE TODAY. . .

HERE IS WHERE I'M STRUGGLING IN MY FAITH. . .

PLEASE ERASE ANY DOUBT IN MY HEART SO THAT. . .

WITH YOU BY MY SIDE, *I know*. . . ..

....

....

....

....

.... *is possible.*

I trust You to. . .

....

....

....

....

....

....

TOGETHER, YOU AND I CAN MOVE THOSE MOUNTAINS, LORD!

Thank You, Father, for hearing my prayers! **AMEN.**

It is better to take refuge in the
Lord than to trust in man.
PSALM 118:8 ESV

Date:

DEAR HEAVENLY FATHER,

I believe mountains can move.

THIS IS WHAT NEEDS MOVING IN MY LIFE TODAY. . .

HERE IS WHERE I'M STRUGGLING IN MY FAITH. . .

PLEASE ERASE ANY DOUBT IN MY HEART SO THAT. . .

WITH YOU BY MY SIDE, *I know. . .*

is possible.

I trust You to. . .

TOGETHER, YOU AND I CAN MOVE THOSE MOUNTAINS, LORD!

Thank You, Father, for hearing my prayers! AMEN.

"Come to me, all who labor and are heavy laden, and I will give you rest. Take my yoke upon you, and learn from me, for I am gentle and lowly in heart, and you will find rest for your souls. For my yoke is easy, and my burden is light."

MATTHEW 11:28–30 ESV

Date:

DEAR HEAVENLY FATHER,

I believe mountains can move.

THIS IS WHAT NEEDS MOVING IN MY LIFE TODAY. . .

HERE IS WHERE I'M STRUGGLING IN MY FAITH. . .

PLEASE ERASE ANY DOUBT IN MY HEART SO THAT. . .

WITH YOU BY MY SIDE, I know. . .

is possible.

I trust You to. . .

TOGETHER, YOU AND I CAN MOVE THOSE MOUNTAINS, LORD!

Thank You, Father, for hearing my prayers! **AMEN.**

So let's not get tired of doing what is good.
At just the right time we will reap a
harvest of blessing if we don't give up.
GALATIANS 6:9 NLT

Date:

DEAR HEAVENLY FATHER,

I believe mountains can move.

THIS IS WHAT NEEDS MOVING IN MY LIFE TODAY. . .

HERE IS WHERE I'M STRUGGLING IN MY FAITH. . .

PLEASE ERASE ANY DOUBT IN MY HEART SO THAT. . .

WITH YOU BY MY SIDE, *I know*. . .

is possible.

I trust You to. . .

TOGETHER, YOU AND I CAN MOVE THOSE MOUNTAINS, LORD!

Thank You, Father, for hearing my prayers! **AMEN.**

I have the highest confidence in you, and I take great pride in you. You have greatly encouraged me and made me happy despite all our troubles.

2 Corinthians 7:4 NLT

Date:

DEAR HEAVENLY FATHER,

I believe mountains can move.

THIS IS WHAT NEEDS MOVING IN MY LIFE TODAY. . .

HERE IS WHERE I'M STRUGGLING IN MY FAITH. . .

PLEASE ERASE ANY DOUBT IN MY HEART SO THAT. . .

WITH YOU BY MY SIDE, *I know*. . .

is possible.

I trust You to. . .

TOGETHER, YOU AND I CAN MOVE THOSE MOUNTAINS, LORD!

Thank You, Father, for hearing my prayers! AMEN.

When the righteous cry for help, the LORD hears and delivers them out of all their troubles. The LORD is near to the brokenhearted and saves the crushed in spirit.

PSALM 34:17–18 ESV

Date:

DEAR HEAVENLY FATHER,

I believe mountains can move.

THIS IS WHAT NEEDS MOVING IN MY LIFE TODAY. . .

HERE IS WHERE I'M STRUGGLING IN MY FAITH. . .

PLEASE ERASE ANY DOUBT IN MY HEART SO THAT. . .

WITH YOU BY MY SIDE, *I know*. . .

is possible.

I trust You to. . .

TOGETHER, YOU AND I CAN MOVE THOSE MOUNTAINS, LORD!

Thank You, Father, for hearing my prayers! **AMEN.**

But you, Lord, are a shield around me,
my glory, the One who lifts my head high.
Psalm 3:3 niv

Date:

DEAR HEAVENLY FATHER,

I believe mountains can move.

THIS IS WHAT NEEDS MOVING IN MY LIFE TODAY. . .

HERE IS WHERE I'M STRUGGLING IN MY FAITH. . .

PLEASE ERASE ANY DOUBT IN MY HEART SO THAT. . .

WITH YOU BY MY SIDE, *I know. . .*

is possible.

I trust You to. . .

TOGETHER, YOU AND I CAN MOVE THOSE MOUNTAINS, LORD!

Thank You, Father, for hearing my prayers! **AMEN.**

"Let not your hearts be troubled.
Believe in God; believe also in me."
JOHN 14:1 ESV

Date:

DEAR HEAVENLY FATHER,

I believe mountains can move.

THIS IS WHAT NEEDS MOVING IN MY LIFE TODAY. . .

HERE IS WHERE I'M STRUGGLING IN MY FAITH. . .

PLEASE ERASE ANY DOUBT IN MY HEART SO THAT. . .

WITH YOU BY MY SIDE, I know. . .

is possible.

I trust You to. . .

TOGETHER, YOU AND I CAN MOVE THOSE MOUNTAINS, LORD!

Thank You, Father, for hearing my prayers! **AMEN.**

Leave all your worries with him,
because he cares for you.
1 PETER 5:7 GNT

Date:

DEAR HEAVENLY FATHER,

I believe mountains can move.

THIS IS WHAT NEEDS MOVING IN MY LIFE TODAY. . .

HERE IS WHERE I'M STRUGGLING IN MY FAITH. . .

PLEASE ERASE ANY DOUBT IN MY HEART SO THAT. . .

WITH YOU BY MY SIDE, *I know. . .*

is possible.

I trust You to. . .

TOGETHER, YOU AND I CAN MOVE THOSE MOUNTAINS, LORD!

Thank You, Father, for hearing my prayers! **AMEN.**

Keep company with the wise and you will become wise.

PROVERBS 13:20 GNT

Date:

DEAR HEAVENLY FATHER,

I believe mountains can move.

THIS IS WHAT NEEDS MOVING IN MY LIFE TODAY. . .

HERE IS WHERE I'M STRUGGLING IN MY FAITH. . .

PLEASE ERASE ANY DOUBT IN MY HEART SO THAT. . .

WITH YOU BY MY SIDE, *I know. . .*

is possible.

I trust You to. . .

TOGETHER, YOU AND I CAN MOVE THOSE MOUNTAINS, LORD!

Thank You, Father, for hearing my prayers! **AMEN.**

For am I now seeking the approval of man, or of God?
Or am I trying to please man? If I were still trying
to please man, I would not be a servant of Christ.

GALATIANS 1:10 ESV

Date:

DEAR HEAVENLY FATHER,

I believe mountains can move.

THIS IS WHAT NEEDS MOVING IN MY LIFE TODAY. . .

HERE IS WHERE I'M STRUGGLING IN MY FAITH. . .

PLEASE ERASE ANY DOUBT IN MY HEART SO THAT. . .

WITH YOU BY MY SIDE, *I know. . .* ....

....

....

....

....

.... *is possible.*

I trust You to. . .

....

....

....

....

....

....

TOGETHER, YOU AND I CAN MOVE THOSE MOUNTAINS, LORD!

Thank You, Father, for hearing my prayers! **AMEN.**

Come, my young friends, and listen to me,
and I will teach you to honor the Lord.
Psalm 34:11 GNT

Date:

DEAR HEAVENLY FATHER,

I believe mountains can move.

THIS IS WHAT NEEDS MOVING IN MY LIFE TODAY. . .

HERE IS WHERE I'M STRUGGLING IN MY FAITH. . .

PLEASE ERASE ANY DOUBT IN MY HEART SO THAT. . .

WITH YOU BY MY SIDE, *I know. . .*

is possible.

I trust You to. . .

TOGETHER, YOU AND I CAN MOVE THOSE MOUNTAINS, LORD!

Thank You, Father, for hearing my prayers! **AMEN.**

I am a friend to all who fear you,
to all who follow your precepts.
PSALM 119:63 NIV

Date:

DEAR HEAVENLY FATHER,

I believe mountains can move.

THIS IS WHAT NEEDS MOVING IN MY LIFE TODAY. . .

HERE IS WHERE I'M STRUGGLING IN MY FAITH. . .

PLEASE ERASE ANY DOUBT IN MY HEART SO THAT. . .

WITH YOU BY MY SIDE, *I know. . .* ....

....

....

....

....

.... *is possible.*

I trust You to. . .

....

....

....

....

....

....

TOGETHER, YOU AND I CAN MOVE THOSE MOUNTAINS, LORD!

Thank You, Father, for hearing my prayers! **AMEN.**

It is dangerous to be concerned with what others think of you, but if you trust the LORD, *you are safe.*

PROVERBS 29:25 GNT

Date:

DEAR HEAVENLY FATHER,

I believe mountains can move.

THIS IS WHAT NEEDS MOVING IN MY LIFE TODAY. . .

HERE IS WHERE I'M STRUGGLING IN MY FAITH. . .

PLEASE ERASE ANY DOUBT IN MY HEART SO THAT. . .

WITH YOU BY MY SIDE, *I know*. . .

is possible.

I trust You to. . .

TOGETHER, YOU AND I CAN MOVE THOSE MOUNTAINS, LORD!

Thank You, Father, for hearing my prayers! **AMEN.**

A glad heart makes a happy face;
a broken heart crushes the spirit.
PROVERBS 15:13 NLT

Date:

DEAR HEAVENLY FATHER,

I believe mountains can move.

THIS IS WHAT NEEDS MOVING IN MY LIFE TODAY. . .

HERE IS WHERE I'M STRUGGLING IN MY FAITH. . .

PLEASE ERASE ANY DOUBT IN MY HEART SO THAT. . .

WITH YOU BY MY SIDE, *I know*. . .

is possible.

I trust You to. . .

TOGETHER, YOU AND I CAN MOVE THOSE MOUNTAINS, LORD!

Thank You, Father, for hearing my prayers! **AMEN.**

Don't be selfish; don't try to impress others.
Be humble, thinking of others as better than yourselves.
PHILIPPIANS 2:3 NLT

Date:

DEAR HEAVENLY FATHER,

I believe mountains can move.

THIS IS WHAT NEEDS MOVING IN MY LIFE TODAY. . .

HERE IS WHERE I'M STRUGGLING IN MY FAITH. . .

PLEASE ERASE ANY DOUBT IN MY HEART SO THAT. . .

WITH YOU BY MY SIDE, *I know. . .*

is possible.

I trust You to. . .

TOGETHER, YOU AND I CAN MOVE THOSE MOUNTAINS, LORD!

Thank You, Father, for hearing my prayers! **AMEN.**

Therefore, since we are surrounded by so great a cloud of witnesses, let us also lay aside every weight, and sin which clings so closely, and let us run with endurance the race that is set before us.

HEBREWS 12:1 ESV

Date:

DEAR HEAVENLY FATHER,

I believe mountains can move.

THIS IS WHAT NEEDS MOVING IN MY LIFE TODAY. . .

HERE IS WHERE I'M STRUGGLING IN MY FAITH. . .

PLEASE ERASE ANY DOUBT IN MY HEART SO THAT. . .

WITH YOU BY MY SIDE, *I know. . .* ....

....

....

....

....

.... *is possible.*

I trust You to. . .

....

....

....

....

....

....

TOGETHER, YOU AND I CAN MOVE THOSE MOUNTAINS, LORD!

Thank You, Father, for hearing my prayers! **AMEN.**

So these three things remain: faith, hope, and love. But the best one of these is love.
1 Corinthians 13:13 GW

Date:

DEAR HEAVENLY FATHER,

I believe mountains can move.

THIS IS WHAT NEEDS MOVING IN MY LIFE TODAY. . .

HERE IS WHERE I'M STRUGGLING IN MY FAITH. . .

PLEASE ERASE ANY DOUBT IN MY HEART SO THAT. . .

WITH YOU BY MY SIDE, *I know. . .*

is possible.

I trust You to. . .

TOGETHER, YOU AND I CAN MOVE THOSE MOUNTAINS, LORD!

Thank You, Father, for hearing my prayers! **AMEN.**

"My thoughts," says the Lord, "are not like yours, and my ways are different from yours."
Isaiah 55:8 GNT

Date:

DEAR HEAVENLY FATHER,

I believe mountains can move.

THIS IS WHAT NEEDS MOVING IN MY LIFE TODAY. . .

HERE IS WHERE I'M STRUGGLING IN MY FAITH. . .

PLEASE ERASE ANY DOUBT IN MY HEART SO THAT. . .

WITH YOU BY MY SIDE, *I know*. . .

is possible.

I trust You to. . .

TOGETHER, YOU AND I CAN MOVE THOSE MOUNTAINS, LORD!

Thank You, Father, for hearing my prayers! **AMEN.**

"See, God saves me. I will trust and not be afraid. For the Lord God is my strength and song. And He has become the One Who saves me."

ISAIAH 12:2 NLV

Date:

DEAR HEAVENLY FATHER,

I believe mountains can move.

THIS IS WHAT NEEDS MOVING IN MY LIFE TODAY. . .

HERE IS WHERE I'M STRUGGLING IN MY FAITH. . .

PLEASE ERASE ANY DOUBT IN MY HEART SO THAT. . .

WITH YOU BY MY SIDE, *I know. . .*

is possible.

I trust You to. . .

TOGETHER, YOU AND I CAN MOVE THOSE MOUNTAINS, LORD!

Thank You, Father, for hearing my prayers! **AMEN.**

For the word of God is alive and active. Sharper than any double-edged sword, it penetrates even to dividing soul and spirit, joints and marrow; it judges the thoughts and attitudes of the heart.

HEBREWS 4:12 NIV

Date:

DEAR HEAVENLY FATHER,

I believe mountains can move.

THIS IS WHAT NEEDS MOVING IN MY LIFE TODAY. . .

HERE IS WHERE I'M STRUGGLING IN MY FAITH. . .

PLEASE ERASE ANY DOUBT IN MY HEART SO THAT. . .

WITH YOU BY MY SIDE, *I know. . .*

is possible.

I trust You to. . .

TOGETHER, YOU AND I CAN MOVE THOSE MOUNTAINS, LORD!

Thank You, Father, for hearing my prayers! **AMEN.**

There is therefore now no condemnation for those who are in Christ Jesus.

ROMANS 8:1 ESV

Date:

DEAR HEAVENLY FATHER,

I believe mountains can move.

THIS IS WHAT NEEDS MOVING IN MY LIFE TODAY. . .

HERE IS WHERE I'M STRUGGLING IN MY FAITH. . .

PLEASE ERASE ANY DOUBT IN MY HEART SO THAT. . .

WITH YOU BY MY SIDE, *I know. . .*

is possible.

I trust You to. . .

TOGETHER, YOU AND I CAN MOVE THOSE MOUNTAINS, LORD!

Thank You, Father, for hearing my prayers! **AMEN.**

How precious to me are your thoughts, O God! How vast is the sum of them!

Psalm 139:17 ESV

Date:

DEAR HEAVENLY FATHER,

I believe mountains can move.

THIS IS WHAT NEEDS MOVING IN MY LIFE TODAY. . .

HERE IS WHERE I'M STRUGGLING IN MY FAITH. . .

PLEASE ERASE ANY DOUBT IN MY HEART SO THAT. . .

WITH YOU BY MY SIDE, *I know. . .*

is possible.

I trust You to. . .

TOGETHER, YOU AND I CAN MOVE THOSE MOUNTAINS, LORD!

Thank You, Father, for hearing my prayers! **AMEN.**

Set your minds on things that are above,
not on things that are on earth.
COLOSSIANS 3:2 ESV

Date:

DEAR HEAVENLY FATHER,

I believe mountains can move.

THIS IS WHAT NEEDS MOVING IN MY LIFE TODAY. . .

HERE IS WHERE I'M STRUGGLING IN MY FAITH. . .

PLEASE ERASE ANY DOUBT IN MY HEART SO THAT. . .

WITH YOU BY MY SIDE, *I know*. . .

is possible.

I trust You to. . .

TOGETHER, YOU AND I CAN MOVE THOSE MOUNTAINS, LORD!

Thank You, Father, for hearing my prayers! **AMEN.**

You are my refuge and my shield; your word is my source of hope. . . . Those who love your instructions have great peace and do not stumble.

PSALM 119:114, 165 NLT

Date:

DEAR HEAVENLY FATHER,

I believe mountains can move.

THIS IS WHAT NEEDS MOVING IN MY LIFE TODAY. . .

HERE IS WHERE I'M STRUGGLING IN MY FAITH. . .

PLEASE ERASE ANY DOUBT IN MY HEART SO THAT. . .

WITH YOU BY MY SIDE, *I know*. . .

is possible.

I trust You to. . .

TOGETHER, YOU AND I CAN MOVE THOSE MOUNTAINS, LORD!

Thank You, Father, for hearing my prayers! **AMEN.**

Trust in the L*ORD* *with all your heart,*
and do not lean on your own understanding.
PROVERBS 3:5 ESV

Date:

DEAR HEAVENLY FATHER,

I believe mountains can move.

THIS IS WHAT NEEDS MOVING IN MY LIFE TODAY. . .

HERE IS WHERE I'M STRUGGLING IN MY FAITH. . .

PLEASE ERASE ANY DOUBT IN MY HEART SO THAT. . .

WITH YOU BY MY SIDE, *I know*. . .

is possible.

I trust You to. . .

TOGETHER, YOU AND I CAN MOVE THOSE MOUNTAINS, LORD!

Thank You, Father, for hearing my prayers! **AMEN.**

We know that all things work together for the good of those who love God—those whom he has called according to his plan.

Romans 8:28 gw

Date:

DEAR HEAVENLY FATHER,

I believe mountains can move.

THIS IS WHAT NEEDS MOVING IN MY LIFE TODAY. . .

HERE IS WHERE I'M STRUGGLING IN MY FAITH. . .

PLEASE ERASE ANY DOUBT IN MY HEART SO THAT. . .

WITH YOU BY MY SIDE, *I know. . .* ....

....

....

....

....

.... *is possible.*

I trust You to. . .

....

....

....

....

....

....

TOGETHER, YOU AND I CAN MOVE THOSE MOUNTAINS, LORD!

Thank You, Father, for hearing my prayers! **AMEN.**

And those who are peacemakers will plant seeds of peace and reap a harvest of righteousness.

James 3:18 NLT

Date:

DEAR HEAVENLY FATHER,

I believe mountains can move.

THIS IS WHAT NEEDS MOVING IN MY LIFE TODAY. . .

HERE IS WHERE I'M STRUGGLING IN MY FAITH. . .

PLEASE ERASE ANY DOUBT IN MY HEART SO THAT. . .

WITH YOU BY MY SIDE, *I know. . .*

is possible.

I trust You to. . .

TOGETHER, YOU AND I CAN MOVE THOSE MOUNTAINS, LORD!

Thank You, Father, for hearing my prayers! **AMEN.**

"But seek first the kingdom of God and his righteousness, and all these things will be added to you."

MATTHEW 6:33 ESV

Date:

DEAR HEAVENLY FATHER,

I believe mountains can move.

THIS IS WHAT NEEDS MOVING IN MY LIFE TODAY. . .

HERE IS WHERE I'M STRUGGLING IN MY FAITH. . .

PLEASE ERASE ANY DOUBT IN MY HEART SO THAT. . .

WITH YOU BY MY SIDE, *I know*. . .

is possible.

I trust You to. . .

TOGETHER, YOU AND I CAN MOVE THOSE MOUNTAINS, LORD!

Thank You, Father, for hearing my prayers! **AMEN.**

Therefore be imitators of God, as beloved children.

EPHESIANS 5:1 ESV

Date:

DEAR HEAVENLY FATHER,

I believe mountains can move.

THIS IS WHAT NEEDS MOVING IN MY LIFE TODAY. . .

HERE IS WHERE I'M STRUGGLING IN MY FAITH. . .

PLEASE ERASE ANY DOUBT IN MY HEART SO THAT. . .

WITH YOU BY MY SIDE, *I know*. . .

is possible.

I trust You to. . .

TOGETHER, YOU AND I CAN MOVE THOSE MOUNTAINS, LORD!

Thank You, Father, for hearing my prayers! **AMEN.**

But you belong to God, my dear children. You have already won a victory over those people, because the Spirit who lives in you is greater than the spirit who lives in the world.

1 JOHN 4:4 NLT

Date:

DEAR HEAVENLY FATHER,

I believe mountains can move.

THIS IS WHAT NEEDS MOVING IN MY LIFE TODAY. . .

HERE IS WHERE I'M STRUGGLING IN MY FAITH. . .

PLEASE ERASE ANY DOUBT IN MY HEART SO THAT. . .

WITH YOU BY MY SIDE, *I know. . .*

is possible.

I trust You to. . .

TOGETHER, YOU AND I CAN MOVE THOSE MOUNTAINS, LORD!

Thank You, Father, for hearing my prayers! **AMEN.**

I have been crucified with Christ. It is no longer I who live, but Christ who lives in me. And the life I now live in the flesh I live by faith in the Son of God, who loved me and gave himself for me.

GALATIANS 2:20 ESV

Date:

DEAR HEAVENLY FATHER,

I believe mountains can move.

THIS IS WHAT NEEDS MOVING IN MY LIFE TODAY. . .

HERE IS WHERE I'M STRUGGLING IN MY FAITH. . .

PLEASE ERASE ANY DOUBT IN MY HEART SO THAT. . .

WITH YOU BY MY SIDE, *I know*. . .

is possible.

I trust You to. . .

TOGETHER, YOU AND I CAN MOVE THOSE MOUNTAINS, LORD!

Thank You, Father, for hearing my prayers! **AMEN.**

For the Lord *will be your confidence and will keep your foot from being caught.*
Proverbs 3:26 esv

Date:

DEAR HEAVENLY FATHER,

I believe mountains can move.

THIS IS WHAT NEEDS MOVING IN MY LIFE TODAY. . .

HERE IS WHERE I'M STRUGGLING IN MY FAITH. . .

PLEASE ERASE ANY DOUBT IN MY HEART SO THAT. . .

WITH YOU BY MY SIDE, *I know*. . .

is possible.

I trust You to. . .

TOGETHER, YOU AND I CAN MOVE THOSE MOUNTAINS, LORD!

Thank You, Father, for hearing my prayers! AMEN.

"Be still, and know that I am God. I will be exalted among the nations, I will be exalted in the earth!"

PSALM 46:10 ESV

Date:

DEAR HEAVENLY FATHER,

I believe mountains can move.

THIS IS WHAT NEEDS MOVING IN MY LIFE TODAY. . .

HERE IS WHERE I'M STRUGGLING IN MY FAITH. . .

PLEASE ERASE ANY DOUBT IN MY HEART SO THAT. . .

WITH YOU BY MY SIDE, *I know*. . .

is possible.

I trust You to. . .

TOGETHER, YOU AND I CAN MOVE THOSE MOUNTAINS, LORD!

Thank You, Father, for hearing my prayers! **AMEN.**

My heart is confident in you, O God; my heart is confident. No wonder I can sing your praises!

PSALM 57:7 NLT

Date:

DEAR HEAVENLY FATHER,

I believe mountains can move.

THIS IS WHAT NEEDS MOVING IN MY LIFE TODAY. . .

HERE IS WHERE I'M STRUGGLING IN MY FAITH. . .

PLEASE ERASE ANY DOUBT IN MY HEART SO THAT. . .

WITH YOU BY MY SIDE, *I know*. . .

is possible.

I trust You to. . .

TOGETHER, YOU AND I CAN MOVE THOSE MOUNTAINS, LORD!

Thank You, Father, for hearing my prayers! **AMEN.**

Rejoice in our confident hope.
Be patient in trouble, and keep on praying.
ROMANS 12:12 NLT

Date:

DEAR HEAVENLY FATHER,

I believe mountains can move.

THIS IS WHAT NEEDS MOVING IN MY LIFE TODAY. . .

HERE IS WHERE I'M STRUGGLING IN MY FAITH. . .

PLEASE ERASE ANY DOUBT IN MY HEART SO THAT. . .

WITH YOU BY MY SIDE, *I know*. . .

is possible.

I trust You to. . .

TOGETHER, YOU AND I CAN MOVE THOSE MOUNTAINS, LORD!

Thank You, Father, for hearing my prayers! **AMEN.**

As for me, I look to the Lord for help.
I wait confidently for God to save me,
and my God will certainly hear me.

Micah 7:7 NLT

Date:

DEAR HEAVENLY FATHER,

I believe mountains can move.

THIS IS WHAT NEEDS MOVING IN MY LIFE TODAY. . .

HERE IS WHERE I'M STRUGGLING IN MY FAITH. . .

PLEASE ERASE ANY DOUBT IN MY HEART SO THAT. . .

WITH YOU BY MY SIDE, I know. . .

is possible.

I trust You to. . .

TOGETHER, YOU AND I CAN MOVE THOSE MOUNTAINS, LORD!

Thank You, Father, for hearing my prayers! AMEN.

Because of our faith, Christ has brought us
into this place of undeserved privilege where
we now stand, and we confidently and joyfully
look forward to sharing God's glory.

ROMANS 5:2 NLT

Date:

DEAR HEAVENLY FATHER,

I believe mountains can move.

THIS IS WHAT NEEDS MOVING IN MY LIFE TODAY. . .

HERE IS WHERE I'M STRUGGLING IN MY FAITH. . .

PLEASE ERASE ANY DOUBT IN MY HEART SO THAT. . .

WITH YOU BY MY SIDE, *I know*. . .

is possible.

I trust You to. . .

TOGETHER, YOU AND I CAN MOVE THOSE MOUNTAINS, LORD!

Thank You, Father, for hearing my prayers! **AMEN.**

But if we look forward to something we don't yet have, we must wait patiently and confidently.

ROMANS 8:25 NLT

Date:

DEAR HEAVENLY FATHER,

I believe mountains can move.

THIS IS WHAT NEEDS MOVING IN MY LIFE TODAY. . .

HERE IS WHERE I'M STRUGGLING IN MY FAITH. . .

PLEASE ERASE ANY DOUBT IN MY HEART SO THAT. . .

WITH YOU BY MY SIDE, *I know. . .* ....

....

....

....

....

.... *is possible.*

I trust You to. . .

....

....

....

....

....

....

TOGETHER, YOU AND I CAN MOVE THOSE MOUNTAINS, LORD!

Thank You, Father, for hearing my prayers! **AMEN.**

I pray that God, the source of hope, will fill you completely with joy and peace because you trust in him. Then you will overflow with confident hope through the power of the Holy Spirit.

ROMANS 15:13 NLT

Date:

DEAR HEAVENLY FATHER,

I believe mountains can move.

THIS IS WHAT NEEDS MOVING IN MY LIFE TODAY. . .

HERE IS WHERE I'M STRUGGLING IN MY FAITH. . .

PLEASE ERASE ANY DOUBT IN MY HEART SO THAT. . .

WITH YOU BY MY SIDE, *I know. . .*

is possible.

I trust You to. . .

TOGETHER, YOU AND I CAN MOVE THOSE MOUNTAINS, LORD!

Thank You, Father, for hearing my prayers! **AMEN.**

Then you will be able to live as the Lord wants and will always do what pleases him. Your lives will produce all kinds of good deeds, and you will grow in your knowledge of God.

COLOSSIANS 1:10 GNT

Date:

DEAR HEAVENLY FATHER,

I believe mountains can move.

THIS IS WHAT NEEDS MOVING IN MY LIFE TODAY. . .

HERE IS WHERE I'M STRUGGLING IN MY FAITH. . .

PLEASE ERASE ANY DOUBT IN MY HEART SO THAT. . .

WITH YOU BY MY SIDE, *I know. . .*

is possible.

I trust You to. . .

TOGETHER, YOU AND I CAN MOVE THOSE MOUNTAINS, LORD!

Thank You, Father, for hearing my prayers! **AMEN.**

For where your treasure is,
there will your heart be also.
LUKE 12:34 ESV

Date:

DEAR HEAVENLY FATHER,

I believe mountains can move.

THIS IS WHAT NEEDS MOVING IN MY LIFE TODAY. . .

HERE IS WHERE I'M STRUGGLING IN MY FAITH. . .

PLEASE ERASE ANY DOUBT IN MY HEART SO THAT. . .

WITH YOU BY MY SIDE, *I know...*

is possible.

I trust You to...

TOGETHER, YOU AND I CAN MOVE THOSE MOUNTAINS, LORD!

Thank You, Father, for hearing my prayers! **AMEN.**

In all these things we are more than conquerors through him who loved us.

ROMANS 8:37 ESV

Date:

DEAR HEAVENLY FATHER,

I believe mountains can move.

THIS IS WHAT NEEDS MOVING IN MY LIFE TODAY. . .

HERE IS WHERE I'M STRUGGLING IN MY FAITH. . .

PLEASE ERASE ANY DOUBT IN MY HEART SO THAT. . .

WITH YOU BY MY SIDE, *I know*. . . ..

....

....

....

....

.... *is possible.*

I trust You to. . .

....

....

....

....

....

....

TOGETHER, YOU AND I CAN MOVE THOSE MOUNTAINS, LORD!

Thank You, Father, for hearing my prayers! **AMEN.**

Shout for joy to the Lord, *all the earth. Worship the* Lord *with gladness; come before him with joyful songs. Know that the* Lord *is God. It is he who made us, and we are his; we are his people, the sheep of his pasture.*

Psalm 100:1–3 NIV

Date:

DEAR HEAVENLY FATHER,

I believe mountains can move.

THIS IS WHAT NEEDS MOVING IN MY LIFE TODAY. . .

HERE IS WHERE I'M STRUGGLING IN MY FAITH. . .

PLEASE ERASE ANY DOUBT IN MY HEART SO THAT. . .

WITH YOU BY MY SIDE, *I know*. . .

is possible.

I trust You to. . .

TOGETHER, YOU AND I CAN MOVE THOSE MOUNTAINS, LORD!

Thank You, Father, for hearing my prayers! **AMEN.**

For we are his workmanship, created in Christ Jesus for good works, which God prepared beforehand, that we should walk in them.

EPHESIANS 2:10 ESV

Date:

DEAR HEAVENLY FATHER,

I believe mountains can move.

THIS IS WHAT NEEDS MOVING IN MY LIFE TODAY. . .

HERE IS WHERE I'M STRUGGLING IN MY FAITH. . .

PLEASE ERASE ANY DOUBT IN MY HEART SO THAT. . .

WITH YOU BY MY SIDE, *I know*. . .

is possible.

I trust You to. . .

TOGETHER, YOU AND I CAN MOVE THOSE MOUNTAINS, LORD!

Thank You, Father, for hearing my prayers! **AMEN.**

For I am not ashamed of this Good News about Christ. It is the power of God at work, saving everyone who believes—the Jew first and also the Gentile.

ROMANS 1:16 NLT

Date:

DEAR HEAVENLY FATHER,

I believe mountains can move.

THIS IS WHAT NEEDS MOVING IN MY LIFE TODAY. . .

HERE IS WHERE I'M STRUGGLING IN MY FAITH. . .

PLEASE ERASE ANY DOUBT IN MY HEART SO THAT. . .

WITH YOU BY MY SIDE, *I know* . . .

is possible.

I trust You to. . .

TOGETHER, YOU AND I CAN MOVE THOSE MOUNTAINS, LORD!

Thank You, Father, for hearing my prayers! **AMEN.**

He put a new song in my mouth, a song of praise to our God. Many will see and fear, and put their trust in the LORD.

PSALM 40:3 ESV

Date:

DEAR HEAVENLY FATHER,

I believe mountains can move.

THIS IS WHAT NEEDS MOVING IN MY LIFE TODAY. . .

HERE IS WHERE I'M STRUGGLING IN MY FAITH. . .

PLEASE ERASE ANY DOUBT IN MY HEART SO THAT. . .

WITH YOU BY MY SIDE, I know. . .

is possible.

I trust You to. . .

TOGETHER, YOU AND I CAN MOVE THOSE MOUNTAINS, LORD!

Thank You, Father, for hearing my prayers! **AMEN.**

Count it all joy, my brothers, when you meet trials of various kinds, for you know that the testing of your faith produces steadfastness. And let steadfastness have its full effect, that you may be perfect and complete, lacking in nothing.

JAMES 1:2–4 ESV

Date: ....

DEAR HEAVENLY FATHER, ...

I believe mountains can move.

THIS IS WHAT NEEDS MOVING IN MY LIFE TODAY. . .

HERE IS WHERE I'M STRUGGLING IN MY FAITH. . .

PLEASE ERASE ANY DOUBT IN MY HEART SO THAT. . .

WITH YOU BY MY SIDE, *I know*. . .

is possible.

I trust You to. . .

TOGETHER, YOU AND I CAN MOVE THOSE MOUNTAINS, LORD!

Thank You, Father, for hearing my prayers! **AMEN.**

*And after you have suffered a little while,
the God of all grace, who has called you to
his eternal glory in Christ, will himself restore,
confirm, strengthen, and establish you.*

1 PETER 5:10 ESV

Date:

DEAR HEAVENLY FATHER,

I believe mountains can move.

THIS IS WHAT NEEDS MOVING IN MY LIFE TODAY. . .

HERE IS WHERE I'M STRUGGLING IN MY FAITH. . .

PLEASE ERASE ANY DOUBT IN MY HEART SO THAT. . .

WITH YOU BY MY SIDE, I know. . .

is possible.

I trust You to. . .

TOGETHER, YOU AND I CAN MOVE THOSE MOUNTAINS, LORD!

Thank You, Father, for hearing my prayers! AMEN.

You love him, although you have not seen him, and you believe in him, although you do not now see him. So you rejoice with a great and glorious joy which words cannot express, because you are receiving the salvation of your souls, which is the purpose of your faith in him.

1 PETER 1:8–9 GNT

Date:

DEAR HEAVENLY FATHER,

I believe mountains can move.

THIS IS WHAT NEEDS MOVING IN MY LIFE TODAY. . .

HERE IS WHERE I'M STRUGGLING IN MY FAITH. . .

PLEASE ERASE ANY DOUBT IN MY HEART SO THAT. . .

WITH YOU BY MY SIDE, *I know*. . .

is possible.

I trust You to. . .

TOGETHER, YOU AND I CAN MOVE THOSE MOUNTAINS, LORD!

Thank You, Father, for hearing my prayers! **AMEN.**

What then shall we say to these things?
If God is for us, who can be against us?
ROMANS 8:31 ESV

Discover More Faith Maps for the Entire Family. . .

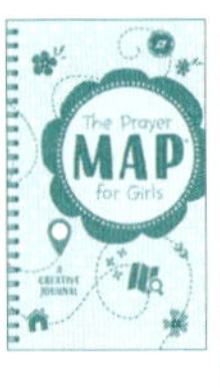

The Prayer Map for Men
978-1-64352-438-2

The Prayer Map for Women
978-1-63609-762-6
978-1-63609-763-3

The Prayer Map for Girls
978-1-68322-559-1

The Prayer Map for Boys
978-1-68322-558-4

The Prayer Map for Teens
978-1-68322-556-0

The Prayer Map for Teen Girls
978-1-63609-803-6

These purposeful prayer journals are a fun and creative way to experience the power of prayer more fully. Each page guides you to write out thoughts, ideas, and lists. . .creating a specific "map" for you to follow as you talk to God. Each map includes a spot to record the date, so you can look back on your prayers and see how God has worked in your life. *The Prayer Map* will not only encourage you to spend time talking with God about the things that matter most. . .it will also help you build a healthy spiritual habit of continual prayer for life!

Find These and More from Barbour Books or at Your Favorite Bookstore or www.barbourbooks.com